FRAGRANT AFRICAN FLOWERS

poems by

Antonia Apolinario

Hazel Bell

Maryetta Kelsick Boose

Shirley Dougan

Hazel Clayton Harrison

Cynthia Williams

Nancy Ellen Webb Williams

Ginny Knight, editor
drawings and cover design by Ginny Knight

GUILD PRESS
P.O. Box 22583
Robbinsdale, MN
55422

FRAGRANT AFRICAN FLOWERS
was made possible in part
by assistance from
Larson Publications, Osseo, Minnesota.

International Standard Book Number 0-940248-36-0
Library Of Congress Catalog Card Number 89-83645
Copyright © 1989 Guild Press

ALL RIGHTS RESERVED
Reproduction in whole or in part without written permission is prohibited,
except by a reviewer who may quote brief passages in a review.

CONTENTS

Introduction by Ginny Knight   page 1

Antonia Apolinario   pages 3 - 9
- TO ENDURE
- IMMIGRANT
- A PEDRA (The Rock)
- FOR MY NEIGHBOR IN THE CITY
- A CIRANDA
- MY PROMISED LAND
- AMERICAN FARM WOMAN
- PIXOTE DID NOT DIE
- SEARCHING

Hazel Bell   pages 10 - 16
- AFRICA: THE VISIT HOME
- A SURE THING
- SOUL FOOD
- GOD'S HANDIWORK
- WALKIN' AND TALKIN'
- "BIGMOMMA"
- ON THE WINGS OF THEIR HOPES
- CONSUMERS
- BODY LANGUAGE
- REPEAT PERFORMANCE
- REALITY
- THE BEGINNING OF LIGHT

Maryetta Kelsick Boose   pages 17 - 23
- OH JAMAICA
- YOUNG GIRL FISHING
- MEETING A DREADLOCK
- LINGERING THERE
- SHOWING THE BLOOD
- WAVES
- HOME OF MY FATHER'S FATHER
- THE GREAT RIVER
- THE BRIDGE
- SOUTH AFRICA
- SHE DEFIED THEM
- I'M NOT DONE

Shirley Dougan   pages 24 - 30
- WATER ON THE MOON
- THOUGH MILES APART
- MOTHER TO SON
- ROCKER
- CALIFORNIA DREAMER
- USED AND ABUSED
- SOJOURN
- SISTER TALK AT CYNTHIA'S HOUSE

Hazel Clayton Harrison   pages 31 - 37
- FRAGRANT AFRICAN FLOWERS
- THE BOOK LOVER
- FALL IN SOUTHERN CALIFORNIA
- WIND CHILD
- KENT STATE MASSACRE
- ON EAST BONDS STREET
- PORTRAIT OF MY FATHER
- TO ANGELA DAVIS
- LOVE EQUATION

Cynthia Williams   pages 38 - 44
- IT DO HELP
- WAIT FOR ME
- WISHING STAR
- DO ME A FAVOR ADAM
- MY MOTHER'S HOUSE
- SMALL EYE
- JOY COMES AFTER
- MISSING THE GOOD TIMES
- AFTER I GET BACK FROM GOING CRAZY

Nancy Ellen Webb Williams   pages 45 - 51
- STRANGERS
- ODE TO MY MUSE
- WHEN UP IS DOWN
- SUPERSTITIONS
- GRANNY JENNY
- BOUT THAT MELTIN POT NOTION
- EXPERIENCE
- WHO COOKED THE CHITT'LINS?
- TRUTH
- STICKIN TO VASELINE
- TIME CLOSES THE DOOR
- THE END
- MY MIND'S BEAUTY

Antonia Apolinario

Hazel Bell

Maryetta Kelsick Boose

Shirley Dougan

Hazel Clayton Harrison

Cynthia Williams

Nancy Ellen Webb Williams

These women remind me of the flowers of Africa — their roots grow deep and strong; their stems are resilient, tough and covered with protective prickles; they bloom fragile, colorful, fragrant blossoms — together, they make a beautiful bouquet of Fragrant African Flowers.

Ginny Knight, editor

Antonia Apolinario

Maryetta Kelsick Boose   Cynthia Williams

Nancy Ellen   Hazel Clayton
 Webb Williams   Harrison

Hazel Bell   Shirley Dougan

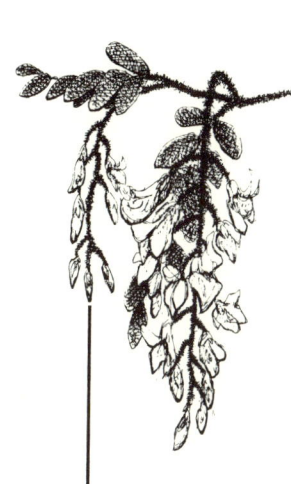

ANTONIA MARIA JORGE APOLINARIO

was born in the "coffee-growing and catfish town" of São Mateus and raised on the island of Vitoria on the coast of Brazil. After moving to Minneapolis with her American husband, in winter she misses "the sun, the ocean's salty smell and the groan of the ship's horns coming into the harbor. When I write, I am transported back home. The sounds of the laughter of kids playing soccer or skipping rope in dusty yards, the chatter of the women balancing kerosene cans of water on their heads, the sweet smell of caramel for the flan, the bright sunshine — all come alive. I miss home then. But when I am home, I miss Minnesota. Writing helps me ease the dilemma."

TO ENDURE

We must be like
    branches
    that bow to the fury
    of the wind
and yet
    still remain
    attached
    to the mother tree

Antonia Apolinario

IMMIGRANT

I thought I was stepping into a
        dream country —
Kennedy airport
        your doors open like magic
        your pop machines are fantastic
you all look so neat and bright
your english is beautiful
        just like in the big screen movies

You said, "Come to America"
Oh how I had dreamed of this land
and the virtues you sold me
        in big bright letters —
            freedom
            opportunity
            equality

Now when we meet for the first time
        you don't recognize me
        your "melting pot" is full
        I am competition for your jobs
you do not welcome me with open arms
I am rudely awakened from my dreams

Antonia Apolinario

A PEDRA (The Rock)

I remember the pedra
as the rocky hill behind our house
where I used to sit in the midday sun
to watch ships and tug boats
come into the bay for iron ore and coffee

I can still feel the warm embrace
that transcends boundaries
      of clothes and skin
warming my soul to a glow

When I sometimes daydream
      I close my eyes
      and I am
            transported
      to the damp salty smell
            in the air
      the aroma of roasted coffee beans
            in the nearby plant
      and hear the longing call
            of the ship's horn

I am brought, thus
      in spirit
to the island of Vitoria

Antonia Apolinario

FOR MY NEIGHBOR IN THE CITY

I worry about you this summer
sure, the weather is hot
sure, it feels just like drifting
    doing nothing
    thinking about nothing
letting God take care of everything

Your shirt proclaims
that you're are
    "too cool for school"
your walk informs me
that you are not up
    to much

They have cornered us
in the middle of the city
    we must plan for ways to get up
    we must move forward
it will take more than
    a smooth talk
    a cool smile
    and a cute face

You are not too cool for school
you are not too cool
    for a good paying job

Sort out your stuff
before you swallow it
    or it's gonna be gone

A CIRANDA

I am in a ciranda
       a whirling circle
everyone goes around the ciranda
       the twirling circle

In trying to keep up with them
       I lose sight of their faces
       their bodies
they are all a big blur

And I who thought
       I had them all
       under control

MY PROMISED LAND

My promised land is a place where
       judgment is accepted
       with an understanding smile

where prejudice
       is dismissed with
       a decision to forgive

where a cry for help
       is attended with a warm hug
       an attentive ear

where we celebrate the gift
       of each new day
       keeping faith that a bountiful
       tomorrow awaits.

Antonia Apolinario

AMERICAN FARM WOMAN

She came from the farm
miles away from the
asphalted city
to march to her son's drum

her thickened waist
her plain washed face
and strong hands
are witness of
a worker of the land

she came to reaffirm that,
    in spite of the farm crisis
    the world market
    the food stamps
        that she and her husband
        must depend on,
she has faith in America

to think that her fruits
have fed millions
    all over the world
yet she is not bitter
or disillusioned
    for having been cheated
    by her country
she believed her politician countrymen
who promised
    there would always be
        a good price for harvest

in spite of chaos in her country
she doesn't miss a step
    she has faith in America

Antonia Apolinario

PIXOTE DID NOT DIE

"Newsweek" reserved a space
of about ten lines
to report that
    the young man — not fully adult —
    who stirred our hearts
    portraying the life
    of a homeless juvenile
    in the streets of Brazil
    was shot by
    the São Paulo police

I don't believe that
they killed
    Pixote
he lives in every pivete
on the streets
    and they can't kill them all.

SEARCHING

When I was little
    you were as powerful
        as the thunder
    as revengeful
        as the lightning
    as mysterious
        as the morning dew

I am no longer little
    but my search for your truth
        still daunts me

In my search for enlightenment
I am only adolescing

HAZEL BELL
is a native of Phoenix, Arizona, and earned her B.A. in social work from Arizona State University. She has lived with multiple sclerosis for over 20 years and has developed "the ability to treasure each day as it arrives." She finds it "satisfying to see my words in print — part of the legacy that I will leave to my two sons." She has found her faith in God to be of "special significance, and I go to Him to seek answers for my life." Now on medical retirement, she resumed writing because she "decided it was best to write about certain feelings to get rid of the pain."

AFRICA: THE VISIT HOME

Never dreamed I'd visit my beginnings
had no thought of ever seeing where I came from

Then I heard the drums
and felt the pulsing answer
    from my heart

My ancestors from both shores
    now hold me close

Hazel Bell

A SURE THING

If I stretch out my hand,
    will you be there
If I open up my heart,
    will you care
If I offer my life
    and all my dreams
Will you give me honesty
    or devious schemes
Do I wait for a clue,
    an unspoken sign
Or strike out alone,
    with a sure thing,
        my mind.

SOUL FOOD

What do I need
to feed my body and soothe my soul
    a soft tender touch
    then maybe I won't feel so cold
where can I find it —
        do I look under Lost and Found
is it in the market —
        can I buy it by the pound
maybe if I stop looking
it'll catch me unaware
    yet, waiting tonight
        seems more than I can bear

Hazel Bell

GOD'S HANDIWORK

Singing a duet with the leaves
the wind makes its presence felt
moving through afternoon sunlight
    the birds sing their praises
        rippling waters play hide and seek
            with a boat drifting on the lake
the beauty of a summer afternoon
God's handiwork for all to see

WALKIN' AND TALKIN'

Sometimes I think
    my words have no weight
        then I remember
    my sons learned about Jesus
    from me

Sometimes I wonder
    do they ever really hear me
        then I remember
    our celebration
    on a joyous Easter Sunday

Sometimes I feel
    that satan is winning the war
        then I remember
    late night conversations
    about God's grace

Sometimes I get tired
    of doing all this talkin'
        then I remember
    I can prove it by my walkin'

Hazel Bell

"BIGMOMMA"
(1912-1988)

One can never have too many grandchildren
    is how my mother views life
The more love she gives out,
    the greater amount she receives

Watching my sons with their Bigmomma
I offer a silent prayer of thanksgiving

She is known as the 'rock'
    and lives up to that name
as the children and grandchildren lean
    she bends but never breaks
her wisdom is wondrous
    inside such a gentle soul

ON THE WINGS OF THEIR HOPES

I move easily over paths made smooth
    by my ancestors
Warm in the glow
of their achievements
    I rest for a spell
In the night, their expectations
    light my way
Soaring high   on the wings
of their hopes
I see places they could only dream of
perhaps   my children will live there

Hazel Bell

CONSUMERS

Tourists walking,
    Oohing, gawking.
    Spying, sighing,
    pointing, buying.

Owners hawking,
    yelling, selling.
    Summer's here,
    prices swelling.

Home again, now
what's that for?
I remember now
it reminded me of a star.

Stash it in the closet
    with last year's dreams
    'cause next summer
    we'll buy all new schemes.

BODY LANGUAGE

You still read me like a book
    things you say
    I didn't even know were true
    until you said them
the pull is still there
as my body so quickly
informs me.

Having never seen
my body
as an objective part of me
    I try not to put much
    credence in it.

Hazel Bell

REPEAT PERFORMANCE

My resolve melts
    with the warmth of your kiss
firm decisions disappear in flames
    as I eagerly
      close the space between us

Time has not diminished
    your fire
or your effect on me

Like before
    I offer myself
no strings or conditions attached
    I wonder
      am I a gift?
      or a burnt offering?

REALITY

Nothing is distinct,
    living in the shadows of life
the edges are blurred

Focused on your love,
    seen through the eyes
      of my heart
my perception of life
is sharp — but with
    no dangerous points

Only with the clarity
    of forever
do I discern
    life and love

Hazel Bell

THE BEGINNING OF LIGHT

Night fell upon my spirit
    one bright and sunny day
I looked inside my soul
    and saw clouds, all dark and grey.

The storm was tremendous,
    tossing me up and down
with no raft to cling to
    I feared that I would drown.

From deep inside I battled,
    refusing to give up the fight
and though I lost some loved ones,
    I saw a hint of light.

Now I am resting,
    secure and guiding my ship
I hear the darkness tearing
    and see sunlight
        through the rip.

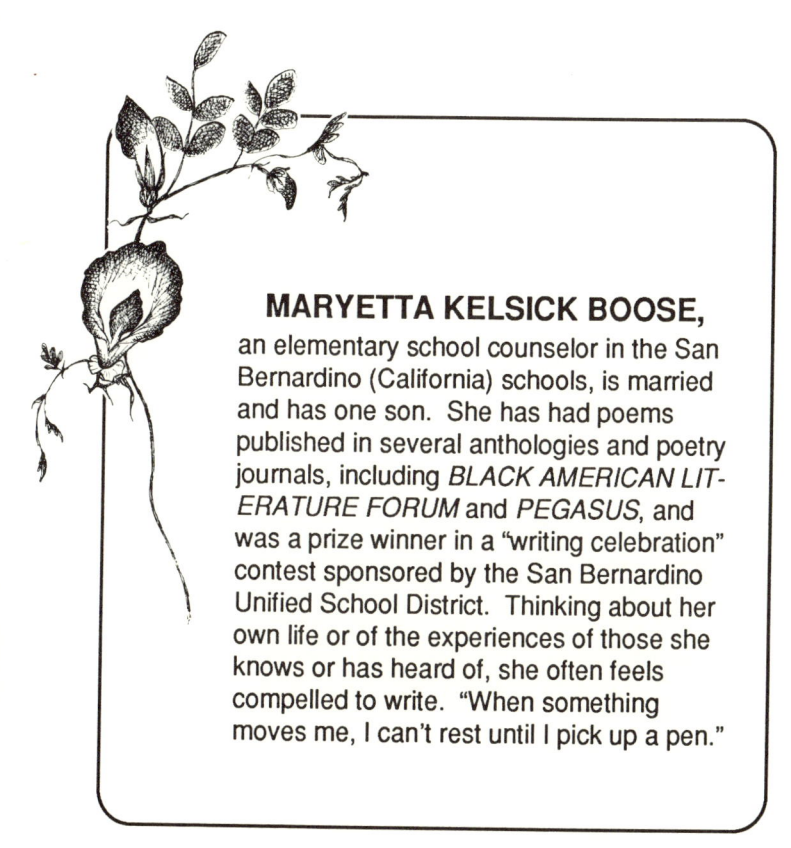

MARYETTA KELSICK BOOSE, an elementary school counselor in the San Bernardino (California) schools, is married and has one son. She has had poems published in several anthologies and poetry journals, including *BLACK AMERICAN LITERATURE FORUM* and *PEGASUS*, and was a prize winner in a "writing celebration" contest sponsored by the San Bernardino Unified School District. Thinking about her own life or of the experiences of those she knows or has heard of, she often feels compelled to write. "When something moves me, I can't rest until I pick up a pen."

OH JAMAICA

Oh Jamaica
I stand on your shores,
sifting the white, white sand
    through my feet
and gaze at your blue-green sea

I feel a kinship
with your sons and daughters —
descendents, like me,
    from Africa.

Maryetta Kelsick Boose

YOUNG GIRL FISHING

Quietly, she stepped —
    eyes determined,
      skirt held out in front
        like a net,
water swishing all around.

Quietly, she circled —
bent her knees
and came up
    with her catch.

MEETING A DREADLOCK

I saw you when I turned the corner.
There you stood on the curb,
your uncombed, twisted hair hanging long.
Wood carvings all around you.

As I looked at your hands' creations,
I watched you out of my eye's corner,
remembering what I read about Dreads
in the paper at home.

You didn't try to sell me ganja
or take hold of my bag
or take me behind a building.

You smiled and spoke of:
    white sand and beaches
    restaurants and rice and peas
    Reggae and Bob Marley
and you sold me wood carvings.

Maryetta Kelsick Boose

LINGERING THERE

At the shop where records
spin round and round,
girls of 15 and 16 years
in blue and white uniforms
linger after school,
snapping their fingers
moving their hips
while their eyes seek
the young man's
    across the room.

SHOWING THE BLOOD

I no longer wanted to look
like a tourist,
    hurrying along in shorts
    or sundress,
    being stopped at every corner
    and shown purses
    mangoes or beads.

So ignoring the heat of the day
I donned a dress with sleeves
and strolled proudly
    along the streets
    answering greetings of
        "mornin' sister"
    and showing the blood
        of my father's
            father.

Maryetta Kelsick Boose

WAVES

Listen!
At night waves pound against the rocks
like hands upon bongos
and in the morning
    tap softly
like a woman's nails
upon a table.

HOME OF MY FATHER'S FATHER

On the veranda I sit
in a white wicker chair
and gaze at the blue-green sea
    of the Carribean
watching the sail boats sway
gently in the wind.

I listen to the waves beat
against the rocks
and hear the distant tune
    of Reggae
    in Jamaica —
home of my father's father.

Maryetta Kelsick Boose

THE GREAT RIVER

I sit and watch the boatmen
smoothly lift the oars as they row
the boat full of people
    from many countries
to a Reggae and Calypso festival.

We pass houses draped in bamboo
children stand and watch us
    glide slowly by.

We pass torches, there to guide
the boatmen along
or to put lovers in the mood
for a kiss   or two.

Down the Great River
    I sit with dreamy eyes
    and folded hands
waiting for the music.

THE BRIDGE

It loomed up at me,
steel on top of steel,
threatening
    to plunge me
    into the dark waters
if I took my eyes away
from its cold, shiny floor.

My hands glisten with sweat,
I grip the wheel
fix my eyes straight ahead
and hope
    the other side will
    hurry up and meet me.

SOUTH AFRICA

Here minorities
      live like movie stars
in homes with swimming pools
wearing diamonds and gold
produced by the backs
      and sweat
      of millions of the majority
who are kept in shacks
      like caged animals.

SHE DEFIED THEM
(For Winnie Mandela)

She defied them —
      standing there before the crowd
      speaking out against those
           who hold her people
           in shackles and chains
      while they rape her Black country.

Again and again
      they dragged her from her home
      tearing away the hands that tried to grasp
      the door of her homeland.

Then they set her outside Johannesburg
      threatening to make sure
      her eyes never again opened
      or her mouth never again moved.

But she returned
      again and again
      and stood
           before her people.

Maryetta Kelsick Boose

I'M NOT DONE
(Reflections on a 43rd birthday)

I'm not done
Like a river
    that flows and flows
I'm not stopping — not yet.

I've opened books for children
    words flowing from my mouth
I've stood for hours
    pushing an iron back and forth
I'm not done.

I've answered lights up and down halls
    emptied bedpans at night
sat in classrooms in the day
    so I could hang three degrees on my wall
I'm not done

I've stood in front of classrooms
    listened to children
    their joys their fears
I've seen my words of poetry
    in journals and books
and I'm still not done

Like a river that flows
    and flows
I'm not stopping — not yet.

SHIRLEY DOUGAN

(Shirley Dougan King) is a native of Chicago. She is the mother of two children, Paul and Charlotte. She is currently teaching in the Minneapolis public school system. In 1987, she co-edited the annual anthology of poetry *FULL CIRCLE EIGHT*. She says writing has been an important part of her life for many years. Her wish is that her poetry will give to others the pleasure it gives to her.

WATER ON THE MOON

Do you see
      the water on the moon?
The deep valleys sparkling
      to the brim
with   sweet, clear water
      kissed by night.

Can you smell
      the sweet fragrance
      of moon water?

Have you ever dipped your cup
into   water from the moon?

Come with me —
      I know a place.

Shirley Dougan

THOUGH MILES APART

Though miles
      apart,
we share the same
sky, moon and stars.

You travel through
the same time
      as I.
Each dawn,
      each sunset
is ours to share.

There are lonely days
when I must be reminded
of what we share —
      days
when bridging the gap
of dawn to sunset
seems more
like a monster
      to conquer
than a time to pass.

Shirley Dougan

MOTHER TO SON

My heart aches,
aches for a time
when smiles and kisses
were free —
       so free.

My heart aches.
It aches for a time
       when trust came
as easy as the confidences
       we shared.

But you're older now.
(it's not that easy
       anymore.)

You push, pull away
       in an effort to find
              your own way.
I hold on in vain efforts
       to still control.

The time has come now
       for new reasons
            to trust.
New confidences to be shared.
       New reasons to love
            mother to son.

Shirley Dougan

ROCKER

The beat of my rocker
    flows
with the pulsing
    of my
        thoughts

Surrounding me
with the rhythms
    of lonely

I know where
we hide loneliness
right to the left
    of imagination
where whimsy
for one moment
    can be real
        to the touch

My need for you
makes me reach out . . .

Once again
my rocker
    beats out
    the rhythms

Shirley Dougan

CALIFORNIA DREAMING

Warm sandy beaches
      so lush I feel
      transported

Ports of call with treasures
      only before
          imagined

My California dreaming finally
      took me there

A balmy night in a seaside
      restaurant
sipping brandy dreaming
of sailing off into
that beautiful sea
      with you
California dreaming
dreaming 'bout you

USED AND ABUSED

I have tried
to label   these feelings
and   in the process
        you
I come up blank.

If only this body knew
words. If only this
passion could be
      put to print.
If only the words
      "I love you"
were not so
      over used.

Shirley Dougan

SOJOURN

Yes morning
          is the worst
          time of day

      I remember
sleep takes me someplace
          I don't know
          I don't feel
with the sun coming
in I remember
          all of you
      your touch, smell
      the way I'm wrapped
around you in the
          fresh day

I remember the peace
      I felt when
walking into that shabby
          place
      your look
that says "you're home
          now"

Yes morning is the worst
          time
my sojourn of remembering
      all of this
          begins again

Shirley Dougan

SISTER TALK AT CYNTHIA'S HOUSE

enjoying the warm crackly fire
with good sisters

not really talking about

earth shaking issues
just Gloria and her
Vander-bilt jeans
    (Who's "built" and who ain't)

we won't solve a lot today

folks will still walk the streets
    homeless
white snow will still mess with many
    minds
but for a little while sisters
    will come together
and harmonize in their own special
    way
sweet music will fill the air
    sweet music
        sweet music of sister
            talk

HAZEL CLAYTON HARRISON, president of her own technical writing, training and consulting firm, lives in Los Angeles with her husband and daughter. Past president of the Los Angeles chapter of the International Black Writers and Artists, she is both a poet and a fiction writer whose writings have appeared in numerous anthologies and journals. In addition, she edited *ON BEING BLACK* and *BEARERS OF BLACKNESS* and co-authored *A MOST DEFIANT ACT* with Ginny Knight. She hopes her writing will help light the way for future generations — "I consider my work to be a testimony to the struggles and survival of my people."

FRAGRANT AFRICAN FLOWERS

Jasmine/Violet/Lily
we are fragrant African flowers,
    scenting the air.
Uprooted from our home,
transplanted in a strange land,
    we seek nourishment
    from rough, rocky soil.
    Yet, we adapt,
    grow strong
    and endure.

Hazel Clayton Harrison

THE BOOK LOVER

After a long, hot day at the office,
I climb in my car and drive
thirty miles in rush hour traffic.

As I reach my exit off
the San Diego freeway
my pulse quickens,
sweat moistens my hands.
I am getting closer to the moment
I have been waiting for all day.

I pull into the garage,
grab my briefcase, leap out of the car,
open the door and rush into the bedroom
to find you still lying on the bed.

Quickly, I pull off my clothes,
climb between the sheets and
pull you close. Gently, I stroke you,
spread your covers wide and
      begin to devour
      every
      word.

Hazel Clayton Harrison

FALL IN SOUTHERN CALIFORNIA

Fall comes reluctantly
to Southern California
like a late summer guest
it arrives on the heels
of gusty November winds
    carrying gifts;
yellow, burgundy, and brown bouquets
of silver maple, heavenly bamboo
and white birch leaves.

WIND CHILD

The wind
is a mischievous little boy
who runs up and down the streets
lifting ladies dresses and
knocking off their hats.

Running through the park
he overturns trash barrels
and plays frisbee with paper plates.

When he grows tired of those games,
he runs off to frolic among
the clouds and play hide and seek
    with the sun
until evening comes
and his mother calls him
    home.

Hazel Clayton Harrison

KENT STATE MASSACRE
(May, 1970)

1.
An army tank blocks the campus
near the charred remains
of the ROTC building.
Unsmiling, helmeted soldiers
look on nervously,
shifting their rifles from shoulder
to shoulder.

Peace settles uneasy
      over the campus
seeping in like tear gas
      so thick
          you could choke on it.
At 10 a.m. a fusillade
(sounding like firecrackers)
interrupts our music class.
      Outside
a white girl runs toward me.
"My God," she cries, "They are killing us."
      An ambulance screams
      Blood stains
          the grass of the commons
          near the student union.

2.
Now a memorial stands
where four were killed.
Children of the protestors
      romp there oblivious
          to the past.
An American flag waves
      red, white and blue fingers
and another page is torn
      from the history book
scattered — leaves
blown across the commons
      by the crying wind.

Hazel Clayton Harrison

ON EAST BONDS STREET

brown skinned Latino boys play
handball   their
shouts/laughter drift
in/out of shadows.

In the driveway, Angela and Chaz
wash my car   their
lips part smiles   hands touch
wax gleams   puddles reflect
    evening scenes
    in quivering mirrors
    on East Bonds Street.

PORTRAIT OF MY FATHER

A pair of faded blue pants
    held up by suspenders,
a tweed cap
    covering a brown moon head
prickley whiskers,
the smell of bourbon and Pall Malls,
hands carved from thirty years
    in steel.
Having served his time in labor camps,
he now enjoys fishing and hunting and playing
    with his
    grandchildren.

Hazel Clayton Harrison

TO ANGELA DAVIS

It must have been hard
    all those years,
    growing up in Birmingham
    knowing the four girls
who were   killed
when the church was bombed.
(Does a child ever forget
the horror of seeing real ghosts?)
It must have been hard
    after studying at
    Brandeis, the Sorbonne,
    learning philosophy and French,
to be hunted by the FBI
    like a dog.
The lies, publicity,
the trial, the expulsion
from UCLA.
You must have thought sometimes
    it wasn't worth it.
But believe me, Angela
it was.
For us   you
were a flame.
We
need you to light
the way.
And we shall continue
to "Lift as we climb"
    onward
for generations
to come.

Hazel Clayton Harrison

LOVE EQUATION

math was simple then.

you plus me equalled one.

with you, i became whole.

i understood the meaning
of yin and yang,
cause and effect,
earth and sky.

don't good things come in pairs?

then you left.

just when i thought i had
it all figured out. now
two minus one equals

nothing.

no matter how many
times i subtract.

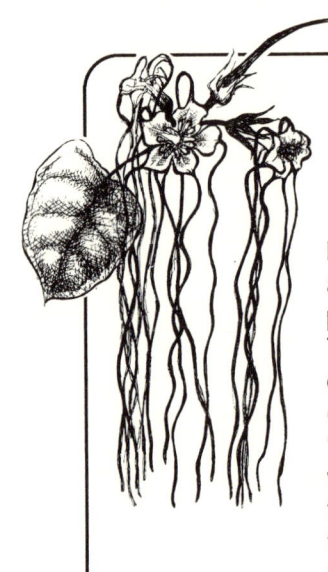

CYNTHIA WILLIAMS
has lived in St. Paul, Minnesota, all of her life. Her poetry has been published in several anthologies. The mother of one daughter, she continually is "seeking ways of experiencing my search" for the "pot of gold" in living, loving, working, playing and praying through words, thoughts and feelings. "Thus do I write — I am hoping to fulfill my prophesy, whatever that may be, and right now God is the only one who truly knows."

IT DO HELP

Wishing won't make it so;
    but wishing is like hoping.

Hoping doesn't make you smile;
    but hoping softens the frown.

Frowning doesn't kill you;
    but it do help!

Cynthia Williams

WAIT FOR ME

Wait for me to catch up
        to where I was before;
which was always
        one step behind
             the rest of the marchers.

That different drummer
        I tried to march to
        didn't even wait;
when I missed that step
        on the half-beat.

This tempo is too fast;
        this beat too difficult.

        Hey you!   Parade!

        I want to march too!

Feet don't trip me up,
        not again.

Wait for me
        please —

Cynthia Williams

WISHING STAR

When you wish
upon a star
    don't
        fall
            off!

DO ME A FAVOR ADAM

Climb up and pick that apple
    for me please
this eve's not made
    for climbing trees

the one I want is near the top
I cannot wait for it to drop

It looks so ripe
    so huge
    so sweet
I know to eat it
    would be a treat

I think I'll cry
    or maybe die
if i can't have the one up high
    it is the apple
        of my eye

Cynthia Williams

MY MOTHER'S HOUSE

Things seemed so uncomplicated
I felt so dedicated
    in my mother's house.

— and until I meditated
over the things
I felt so dedicated about
    finally justifying the reason
    I left that safe, secure,
    care-less existence
— reasoning thus;

        Number one — I wanted freedom;
        freedom to be me
        — independent of a reminder
        that I didn't know
            who "me" was.

        Second, I wanted security
        — the knowledge that
        I can live a thinking, doing,
        loving life,
        and encompass all
            the uncomplicated
            dedicated feelings
            I had in my mother's house.

Please won't someone answer me —
    "What's a nice girl doing
    in a place like this?"

Now, just where did I leave
    my mother's house.

Cynthia Williams

SMALL EYE

Small i laughs at the wind.
Capital U catches it
    as it bounces off the sky.

Capital U smiles at the sun,
small i sits back
    and wonders why?

JOY COMES AFTER

After a long, cold, dismal winter,
    spring comes!

After a tedious, burdensome,
    painful pregnancy
        a child is born!

Does it stand to reason then
    that after losing you
I remember only
    the joy we shared?

Cynthia Williams

MISSING THE GOOD TIMES

Ya, those good times are missing —
I'm missing them and they're missing
me — lately; more and more.

Could it be the good times I remember
are better today than they were yesterday
      the future has passed
      the past is my future?

Could it be also that I forget to enjoy
the good times that are here — today?

I can't remember to forget
what used to be.
I can't forget to remember
what might have been.

Now is forever and today is always today!
Yesterday was always today's sum total
      I can't seem to
      get it together.

— that hexagonal, four-dimensional,
vertical-latitudinal, platitudinous,
lived-in, out-lived life style.

One of these days —
      I'm gonna,
      I gotta —
never again miss
      these good times.

Cynthia Williams

AFTER I GET BACK FROM GOING CRAZY

People tell me I'm slow and awfully lazy
    I'll improve after I get back from going crazy

When sunny days cheer others
    to me they appear to be hazy
I'll see them more clearly
    after I get back from going crazy

When things look glum
when the future seems hopeless
when surprises never come
when I really want to mope less
I tell myself that all will work out
    but until that day, I'll continue to shout

    "These things can wait
    by the garden gate!"

I'll deal with them when
    I get back
        from going crazy!

NANCY ELLEN WEBB WILLIAMS, the fifth of eight children and the mother of three grown children, holds a Master of Public Administration Degree from the University of Nevada, Las Vegas, and is head of the Protective Services Division in the Child Abuse Program of Clark County, Nevada. Under the pen-name "Big Mama" she published the 1986 book of poetry *WHEN WE WERE COLORED*, a poetic look of how it was "before we overcame." She writes to record "the wisdom taught me by The Old Folks" in Quincy, Illinois, her hometown along the Mississippi River.

STRANGERS

Having come from
separate worlds,
my way may not
seem to be your way.

But in the end
I shall not be surprised
    to find
we have traveled different paths
only to make
    the same journey.

Nancy Ellen Webb Williams

ODE TO MY MUSE

Sometimes my Muse
is so laid back,
I know that she
has got to be black.

I say, "Come on now, baby,
help Mama with this line,
you see I been stuck here
a mighty long time."

She say, "Big Mama,
what is dis you say,
I hep you wid
three lines jes yesterday."

"Now ah be restin some
so's ah can take a nap,
and hyear you come
wid yor' brain
all in a handicap."

I say, "Lawdy, baby chile
you know I don't want
to bother you one bit,
but give Big Mama
a hand unknottin' this verse
'cause I can't do nothin' with it."

Ain't more'n a mere
second or two,
Muse get the verse figgured out
to somethin' brand new.

Nancy Ellen Webb Williams

WHEN UP IS DOWN

When up is down
and out is in,
I'll fetch the preacher
to marry us again.

When red takes on
the sorrow of black,
I'll dress in finery
and take you back.

When rocks swim
and turtles fly,
I'll vow to love you
til I die.

SUPERSTITIONS

Screech owl hollerin up the tree.
I know some no-good woman
stole my sweet daddy from me.

Hound dog bayin when nothin's around.
They'll soon be puttin a neighbor
in the cold hard ground.

Lap baby tryin to walk fore his time.
gettin out the way of sister
standin in line.

Circle round the moon
on a warm summer night.
Rain sure to come
and it won't be light.

Nancy Ellen Webb Williams

GRANNY JENNY

Grannie Jenny had fifteen head
    of chillun
by a man she refused to wed.
"Love ain't on no paper,
that's white man's law,"
    she'd say.
"I know who I wants in my bed."

Granny Jenny grabbed her gun
and shot her man for tellin her
too many lies.
    "Warn't fixin to kill him,
    only hurt him a bit.
    It's tween him and God
        if he dies."

BOUT THAT MELTIN POT NOTION

Whitey's got this notion
bout a meltin pot.
    He say
one day the big American kettle
gonna get plenty hot.

Gonna melt down everybody:
    the white, black,
    yellow and red.
Make one single tannish race.
That's what Whitey said.

Now I don't say Whitey's wrong.
    He's usually plenty right.
We'll probably end up one color
    uh-huh
gray ashes behind
Whitey's nuclear fight.

Nancy Ellen Webb Williams

EXPERIENCE

It came from
where it's going

It's been here before.

Experience that has
not taught
goes in and out
the door.

WHO COOKED THE CHITT'LINS?

Who cooked the chitt'lins
for the soul-food banquet?
Who picked em over
and washed em
for the feast?

All the guests are whisperin
these all-important questions.
They need to know the name
of the mystery cook at least.

Chitt'lins be one thing
folks be shy bout eatin,
til they know who
    picked em
    and cleaned em
    for the pot.

Then the cook will testify
    she picked em four hours,
    pulled all the fat out
    and washed em
        an awful lot.

Nancy Ellen Webb Williams

TRUTH

Each word
came with its
grain of salt.

Each offering
tasted bitter.

And yet I knew
the choice was truth
and nothing else
could matter.

STICKIN TO VASELINE

Pretty lady with the accent on TV
sittin there tryin to sell
skin cream to folks like me.
She's not foolin anybody
with that broken-tongue pitch.

I'm stickin to Vaseline;
I ain't about to switch.

She ain't old enough to know
what's really good.
Why she's barely out of
her own childhood.

Sure her skin's smooth and wrinkle-free
but it ain't the cream that done it.
that's plain for all to see.

For all her spiel bout her cream
and its chemistry
its old-time vaseline for me.

Nancy Ellen Webb Williams

TIME CLOSES THE DOOR

Time closes the door
on all that passes
      to open no more.

Yet   he who knows
      this key
understands the past
has   immortality.

THE END

Here we are
      actors as well
      as audience
cast on the screen
of human consciousness
until the end
      silent of applause.

MY MIND'S BEAUTY

Awesome beauty . . .
      grandeur
      like eyes shall never see
gathers sometimes
in my mind
      and quite diminishes
          me.

Some other Guild Press books by women authors

THREE WOMEN BLACK poetry "by three sisters who have something important to say" — Phyllis J. Sloan, Minneapolis; Angela Kinamore, New York; Beverly A. Russell, Los Angeles. "Their voices have impact, their observations are relevant and their wisdom and honesty are inspiring." *ESSENCE MAGAZINE*..
1987   ISBN 0-940248-30-1 $6.00

A MOST DEFIANT ACT poetry by two women, one Black and one White, Hazel Clayton and Ginny Knight. ("Writing a poem can be the most defiant act of all" - Hazel Clayton).
1985   ISBN 0-940248-25-5 $4.50

SURVIVAL: CYCLE OF A BLACK WOMAN includes 33 poets (28 women). Edited by award winning poet Mordecia D. Strickland.
1985 (2nd printing, 1986) ISBN 0-940248-23-9 $5.00

A SAMPLER OF WOMEN Brief biographies of 9 "successful" Minnesota women. Realistic role models for young women of today. Two Black women and one American Indian woman are included. "Well written and beautifully illustrated . . . An excellent resource." - *MINNESOTA REVIEWS*. Large format - 8 1/2 by 11. Easy to read type.
1984   ISBN 0-940248-18-2 $6.50

To order books or for a complete booklist, send your request to:
          Guild Press
          P.O.Box 22583
          Robbinsdale, MN
          55422

NORMANDALE COMMUNITY COLLEGE
LIBRARY
9700 FRANCE AVENUE SOUTH
BLOOMINGTON, MN 55431-4399